Made in the USA
Las Vegas, NV
19 August 2021

28448917R00057